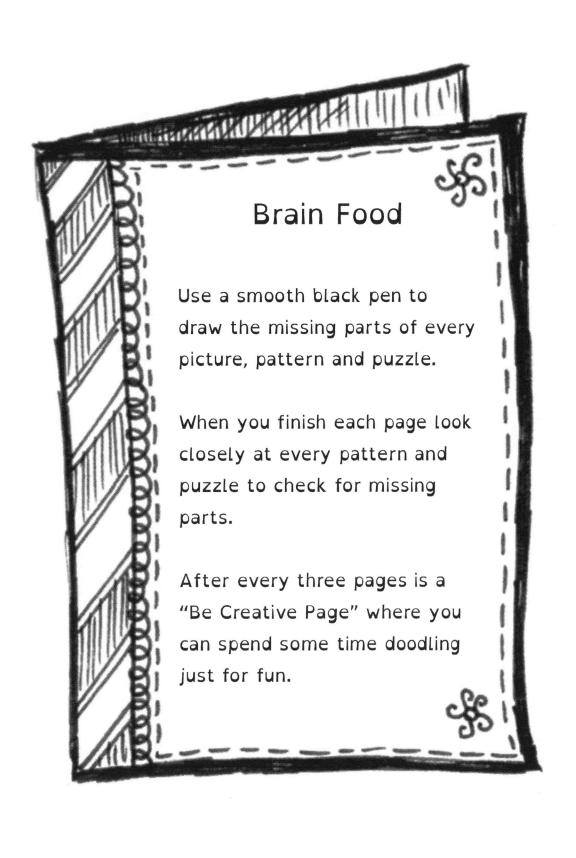

Brain Food

Use a smooth black pen to draw the missing parts of every picture, pattern and puzzle.

When you finish each page look closely at every pattern and puzzle to check for missing parts.

After every three pages is a "Be Creative Page" where you can spend some time doodling just for fun.

What is missing? Write or draw the missing parts!

What is missing? Write or draw the missing parts!

Hot
Tea

Sweet
Honey

Green
Mint

H__
T__

S_____
H____

G_____
M___

Half
&
Half

Fresh
Bread Rolls

F_____
B_____ R_____

H____
&
H____

Green Tea

Warm Muffins

Candy

W___ M_____

It's time to do whatever you want with this page!

Be Creative!

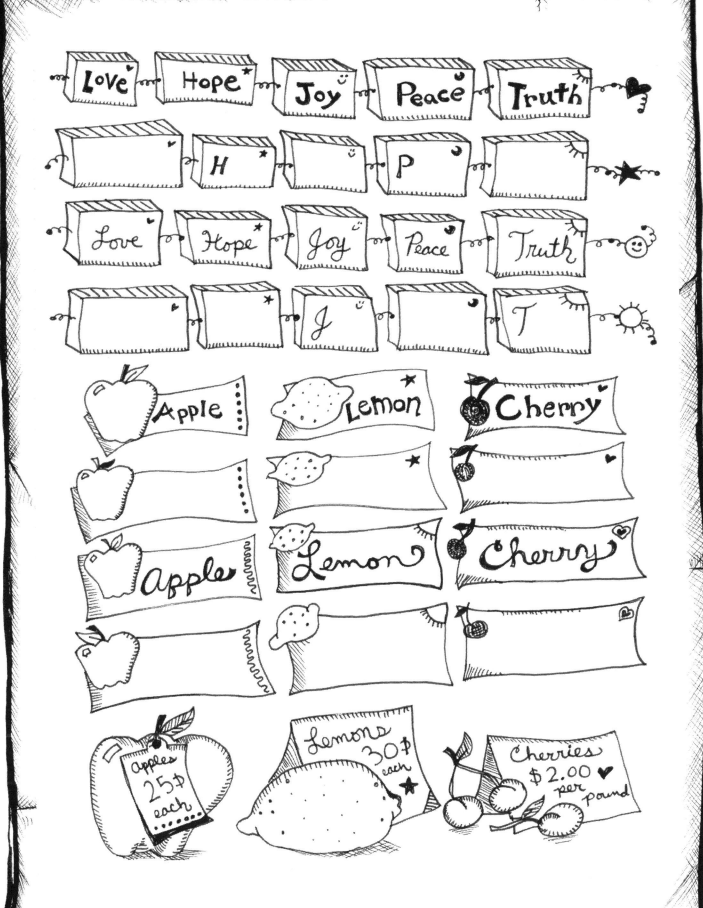

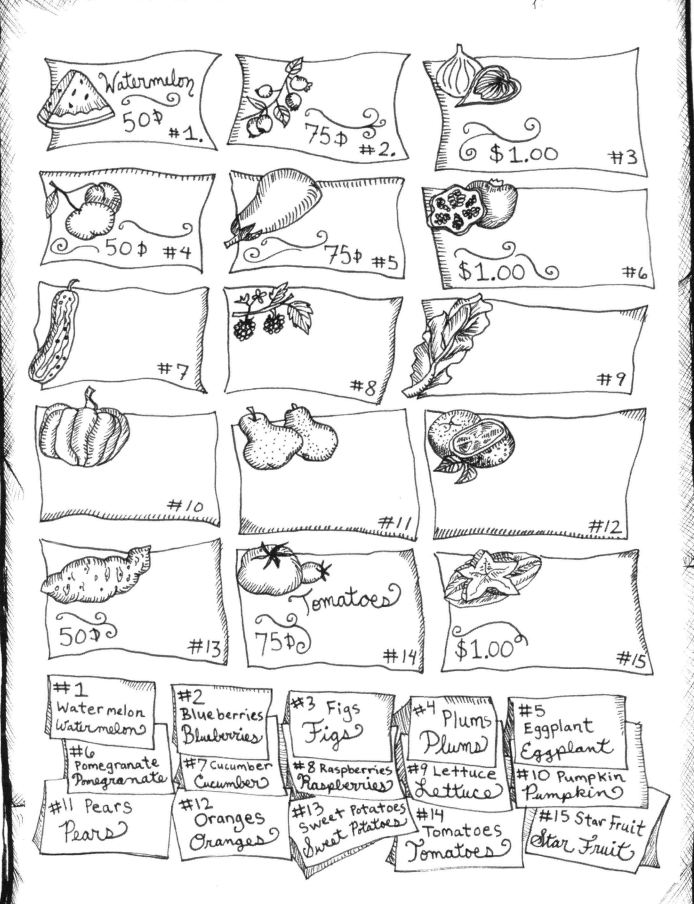

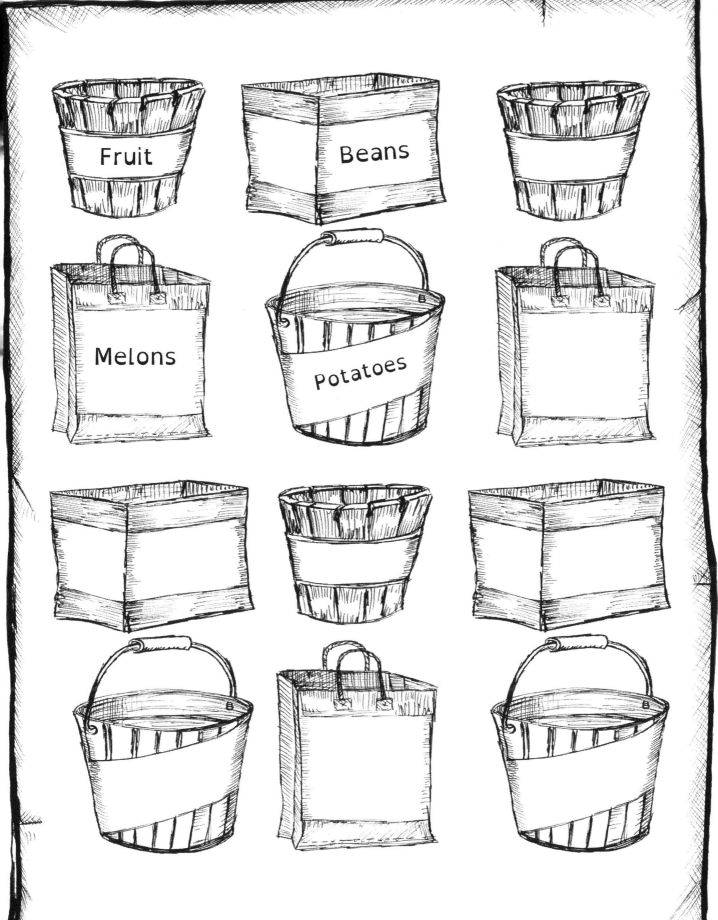

It's time to do whatever you want to with this page!

The Beauty of Fresh Foods

ALMONDS
olives

OLIVES Olives
Olives   Olives

BERRIES

almonds

GRAPES

Almonds

oranges

Berries

grapes

Oranges

cranberries

CRANBERRIES

ORANGES

Cranberries

Figs

Figs

figs

fiGs

carroTs

Carrots

carrots

Eggplant

Cheese

Eggplant

Cheese

Use the blank spaces to practice your Handwriting!

dosh Brown 2015

Be Creative!

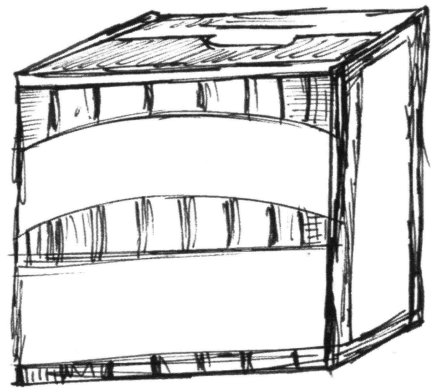

Gift Shop

Bakery

Coffee Shop

Market

Restaurant

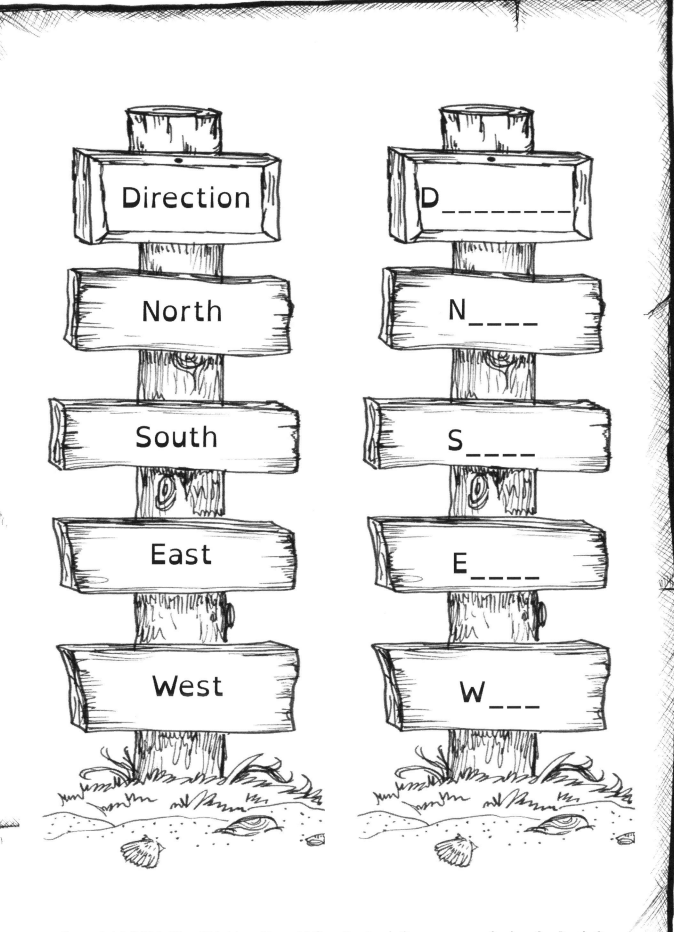

Direction   D_____

North   N_____

South   S_____

East   E_____

West   W____

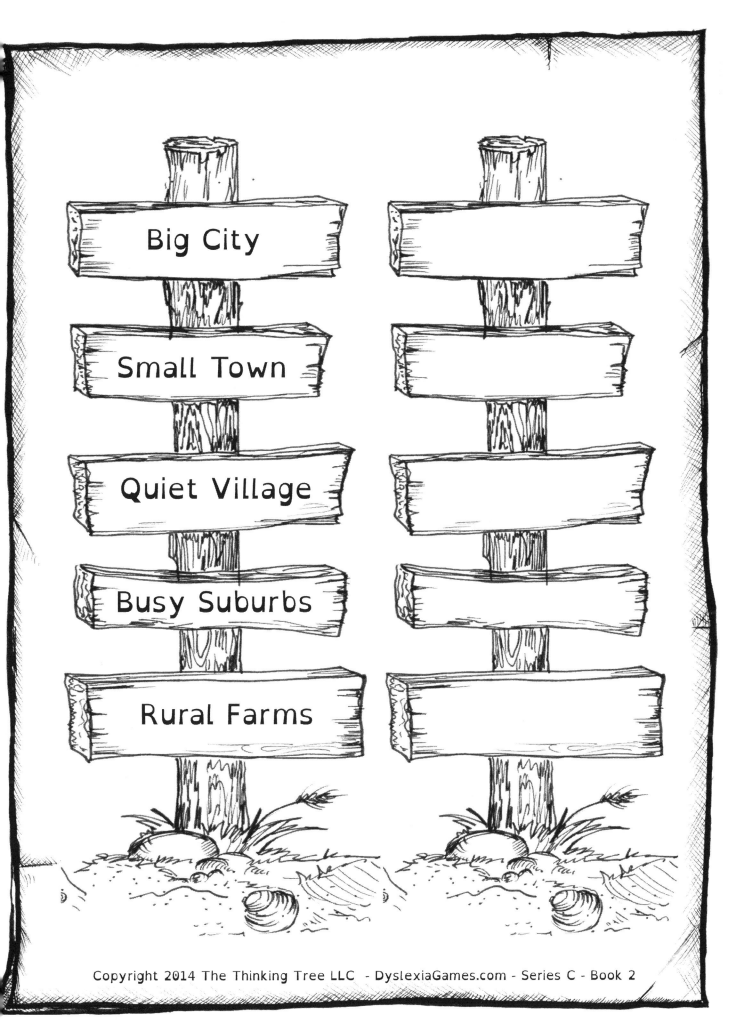

Big City

Small Town

Quiet Village

Busy Suburbs

Rural Farms

It's time to do whatever you want to with this page!

Mountains

M_____

River Valley

R_____ V_____

Farm & Garden

F___ & G_____

Sand & Sea

S___ & S__

Tropical Island

T_____ I_____

Hilltop Village

H_____ V_____

It's time to do whatever you want to with this page!

Be Creative!

Be Creative!

Made in the USA
Columbia, SC
20 October 2018